Sin

Then *and* Now

Sin

Then *and* Now

Biblical Studies in Theology

Dr. Johnny Jenkins Jr.

Sin Then and Now

Printed in the United States of America
ISBN 979-8-89633-033-2 (sc)
ISBN 979-8-89633-060-8 (e)

This book is printed on acid-free paper.

2025.04.24

Page Solutions - Prowriters Network
124 Rock Crystal Ln,
Lakeside Park,
KY 41017A
United States

PAGE
SOLUTIONS
PROWRITERS NETWORK

Sin Then and Now

The debate of Sin and its effect upon mankind is an area under discussion, which people will never come to an agreement. The act or the foundation of sin has mystified even the religious circles. It may stem from the fact they do not want to accept the reason for sin. Or it is possible they can not fathom the idea men, women, boys and girls actions are so out of line with their ways of thinking.

Sin Then and Now has not changed. The method which sin is now being reported has taken on a different path. Mankind will always have a sin-nature as long as he is an occupant of a fleshly body. Yet, we find the reporting of the evils of mankind is more wide-spread throughout the Internet, Television and several other means of communication, which has confused the mass. In order to understand Sin one must understand the Laws of God. If there is no God present, in one's life, he or she will view their actions as not being of major importance. This will cause them to continually descend deeper and deeper into destruction.

Many may ask the question, how can sin be known, if they do not understand or have knowledge of the definition of sin. Let us first define the meaning of sin. Scofield Bible Correspondence Course/Moody gives the definition of sin, in addition to scriptural evidence to confirm the meaning of sin.

(1) Sin is action against, or failure to act in accordance with, the will of God. Rom 3.:23

(2) Sin is a nature. Rom. 5:19

(3) Sin is a state. Rom. 3:9

Moody, therefore, states sin is correctly defined as "any violation of or want of conformity to," the will of God.

To the moralist these definitions should move their entire life appearance to understand that Sin is a great revulsion to the human race. Mankind, including those who are Non-Christians depicted in the afore-mentioned sentence, would like to see these moralists moved to an understanding of sin. History has shown if there is no God in one's culture, mind, body and soul, sin will always be transported with delight as a Christian's way to subdue Man into slavery to a God which they think does not exist.

To the unconverted as well as the converted the acts of sin did not begin yesterday or even with the advent of human governments. Sin, as the Scriptures illustrate, traces its beginning back to one named Satan. The Scripture tells the story of how evil entered into the world and into mankind. The overall acts of evil impregnated mankind with the spirit of disobedience. Because of disobedience, many in the Church age have refused to follow God.

The writings by Dr. Ken Matto-'The Doctrine of Sin-Its Need in the Church', gives wonderful writings on sin as he explains how the church teaches other major doctrines, salvation, justification and others. Yet will shy away from teaching the doctrine of sin and its consequences. This form of teaching is not new; however, if there is a deeper study of the Holy Bible, it can be discovered this form of teaching, whether today or in the past stems from a desire not to offend.

Sin has not changed neither has the way God views sin. Dr. Matto gives four illustrations describing the results of sin and sin's effects on humanity.

(1) Sin Blinds

(2) Sin Causes Us To Stray From The Truth

(3) Sin Diverts

(4) Sin Divides Relationships

Dr. Matto accounts, which are given in these four reasons, gives a description from the beginning of sin in the Garden of Eden to this present time. Because of the devil's deception, in leading Man to eat from the fruit, he has been blinded from the true wisdom of God and his direction in life has been on the downward spiral since. The truth of God and what he requires has escaped man and man looks upon things which seem right in his own eyesight.

Sin then and now, has not simply left the unconverted but also the converted, to wander after his and/or her lustful desires. We want to believe we are immune from the follies of sin; yet, as we observe these acts and the results, it can be shown how no one is immune from sin or from sin's effects. Adam and Eve, the first humans, had the perfect environment and were given a free will to hear the voice of right or wrong and make a choice. They chose to listen to the voice of Satan, who is known to be the author of confusion. Their listening had a devastating effect upon them and the human race. Since they obeyed the wrong voice, God removed them from this wonderful fellowship with him in the Garden of Eden. The outcome of their action caused division with God and their relationship with God suffered. One can see the consequences of their action.

These results, which can be contributed to sin, have been passed down from generation to generation. One of the reasons behind the troubles between humans and their relationship to each other is because of sin. It is strange how theses acts have conquered and divided mankind from generation to generation. The influence of these horrible acts, as Dr. Matto pointed out has moved many people to treat some with respect and some without respect. The acts of favoritism come into play because of sin. It is in the acts of sin, where we find homes with children, jobs, and even churches using these forms of sinful acts for their own selfish reasons.

One should not discount Dr. Matto's analogy of the four illustrations, which describe the results of sin. If a survey were taken, of these subtle sins, it would be seen how common they are from the beginning of time to the present. The religious leaders of old, as well as today, have missed the mark with God which is sin. Sin has led the religious leaders to neglect speaking the word of truth, as God has given it to them, in relationship to sin.

My firm belief is abortion is a sinful act, but many today are into political correctness. This political atmosphere has curtailed their speaking, about abortion. They have also failed to issue a warning about this act. Drunkenness has existed for many years and the Bible speaks about the downfall of much wine; for example, Noah (Gen. 9:21) and it's effect upon him, Lot (Gen. 19: 33) how the act of drunkenness affected him. One who has read and/or will read these accounts and their effects can see why sin must not be treated with a long handle spoon. This politically correct atmosphere, which is prominent today, is not of God, regardless of who presents it. The politically correct people will try to convince people that the soul is free from evil tendencies. This theory gives rise to the Pelagius theory; which is harmful, for it gives man the notion he is not of an evil nature. Those who believe the bible can faithfully prove that political correctness and the Pelagius theory are not of God. To those possessing this way of thinking, they have a goal of blaming evil on a person's low self-esteem instead of blaming sin.

Jesus has shown us how sin is deemed more important than one's self-esteem. "For out of the heart proceed evil thoughts, murders, adulteries, thefts, false witness, blasphemies (Matt.15:19). Where does the low self-esteem theory fit in? My belief is to not contribute sin as the reason for low self-esteem, but the guiltiness that is associated with sin, puts a person into a sorrowful state. The Doctrine of Sin (www.pbministries.org/Theology/simmons/chapter17. htm) illustrates a view of sin, which mankind has been dealing with from the beginning of time. This writing depicts an understanding of sin. The writer will engage its reader to an in-depth view with biblical explanations of the different area of sin in the human race.

1. THE NATURE OF SIN

2. THE UNIVERSALITY OF SIN IN THE HUMAN FAMILY

3. THE EXTENT OF SIN IN MAN'BEING

Those who are struggling, within themselves, of what is right and wrong would be wise to examine this doctrine of sin and its effect on mankind. Man's state will always be in conflict with a Holy God, as long as he is alive in this body. No man, regardless of how hard he tries, will be able to reach perfection down here on earth; for, his blood is tainted with the blood of Adam.

The sin of Adam and Eve involved selfness in the past, as well as today, and is promoted today within the human race. The sin of selfness is based upon man's satisfaction of his own self. Instead of Eve trying to do right with God, she decided it was more important to satisfy her own desires than to do right with God. The first man Adam found himself engaging into the same evil practice. God spoke to him, about sin and its consequences and God said to Adam don't, and Adam said I will. This act was done to satisfy himself and his wife, not God. It was more important to satisfy himself than to be in obedience to God, the one who breathed the breath of life into his nostrils.

Sin is not something which stays the same. My observation of sin can be viewed as a type of progressive cancer, which moves from one act to another. Its job, if not put in check by the power of the Holy Spirit, is to infect the mind, body and soul of all mankind. The unconverted is hopeless without an aide to rely on for his sin, yet we find the saved not using the power of the Holy Spirit to come to rescue; when this deadly disease is overtaking him or her. Let us look at this cancer (sin) as, the Bible points out.

Cancer, as a disease, loves to attach itself to healthy cells and destroy the life of healthy cells by removing the blood. Now, in order to keep living and spreading to other cells, cancer will follow this pattern to make cells just like it. Sin has a tendency to take on the same form with mankind, for if one associates with sin too long; one becomes a lover of these acts and will begin to pass it down to others without remorse For men shall be lover of their own selves, covetous, boaster, proud, blasphemers, disobedient to parents, unthankful, unholy(2Tim.3:2, 4).

If one continues to read these verses and others, the correlation of the disease of cancer and the cancer of sin is prevalent. Medicine is the only thing, which can help a person with cancer endure pain as the body is being attacked. For the Christian, the cancer of sin gets worse as he moves closer to God, and the need for spiritual medication of the Holy Spirit is a daily prescription. Sin has warped the mind of mankind, from creation of Adam, to this present time.

In the beginning, one can see that Adam's mind was on the goodness of God; yet, the moment sin entered into his mind, he became warped and destitute and everything about him began to change (Gen.6:5). His heart, affections, conscience, speech and even his feet were changed. No wonder the Bible says we were all born in sin, how could we not be, when all parts of us have taken on the corrupt blood of the first man. We should not be fooled, by those who try to use their intellect and their great learning, in order to bamboozle us about sin as not being a state, but a conscious choice. Choosing this way is a contradiction against what Jesus said in (Matt.15:19).

The apostasy of Adam has put all men into this category of sin. The Bible, since it is the holy word of God, puts an end to this statement. Wherefore, as by one man, sin entered into the world and death by sin; and so death passed upon all men, for that all have sinned (Rm. 5:12): This gives us an indication, sin is not only a present state, but is somewhat of a then and now problem and man is caught up in its trap.

Let us look at sin and its effects upon our country, and arguments may be rendered, which could be left up to each individual. The United States of America is a country of great advancement in all aspects, from its early existence it has strived to be number one. America is on the verge of reaching a position, in the world, which is not of good standing before the Almighty God. Sin is causing this country to move into a position, that if there is not a great awakening the Roman Empire will be second to America in its fall. Sin, which is missing the mark, has caused God to show America through natural disasters, crime on the streets, disruption in homes and other areas, that it is time to turn back to the one who has blessed you above all other nations.

No one in America can rightfully take the 'I am not the blame' attitude. Our churches must take some blame for a portion of these sinful acts. They have failed to stand for the will of God. Some Churches are more concerned about money and large numbers of people in the pews than what happens to men and women when they leave the pews. The prosperity gospel is a trick of the devil, which blinds men of his or her sinful condition. They have formulated into their hearts and minds money can solve all of their problems. What can be done to cancel out this teaching and the act of sin, which saturates the very fiber of America society? We are aware sin will always be around and if sin is left unchecked, it will have a devastating effect on mankind. The church has a responsibility to preach and teach about sin, to show those in church and out of church the only remedy for this hopeless condition is through the grace of God in Jesus Christ.

I say to those who wish to argue, give me another reason why America is seeing more and more destruction from floods, wild fires etc. Some may say global warming is to blame. One may have an argument, from a scientific viewpoint, my viewpoint is that sin, in America, has moved God to send this country a warning to look within itself and change from its evil ways. How can we, who know God, sit back and refuse to speak out against the sinful acts of rape murder, corporate greed, child molestation and the misuse of authority by those in authority.

The affections of mankind to sin are an on going thing. It is like a fire thirsting for water and to some they just can not get enough of doing the wrong thing. Man's state, he who was born in sin and shaped in iniquity, craves for a desire to sin as much as he can. Regardless, of the price he must pay for his actions, he shows no regard to who it might affect. Death, as a price for sin, is frequently mentioned in the Bible as a penalty for sin. We know God pronounced this judgment upon the first man Adam, and this judgment is still into effect today.

Lehman Strauss, Litt. D., F.R.G.S. (www.Bible.org) in his writing, The Doctrine of Sin points out, "Since sin is a capital crime against God, man is guilty of death." He also gives scriptures to back up his claim to the death judgment upon mankind, (Gen.2:17) to Adam and Eve "In the day that thou eatest thereof, thou shalt surely die, other scriptures are (Ezekiel 18:4), (Romans 6:23) (Heb9:27). It is important that one would engage him or herself, in an in-depth study, of these and other scriptures to see how sin has caused God to pronounce this sentence of death on mankind. Many will ponder, in their minds, of how God who claims to be loving and caring pronounces such judgment of this kind to his creatures. This brings to mind, the excerpt, for every action there is a reaction. When a sinful child does something to sinful parents there is a punishment, which has to be given out to bring one back to the realization this act was wrong. Each time a law of a home is broken, punishment is a necessity. The readers may ask why the words sinful parents were used. The Bible points to the fact we all are sinners. God, as we are aware, is not a sinner. God is loving and kind etc., but we should be constantly reminded, by those who God has appointed over His people that God is also Holy.

They must be willing to explain to the sinner and others, He has a high standard of perfection and when men fail to meet His standard or miss the mark which is sin, God's holiness demands a verdict upon the sinner. There are many who will try to argue their point, of how they have done wrong and did not receive the punishment of death. Adam and Eve believed this lie of the devil, who is the author of sin. He continues to spread lies of deceitfulness, in order to confuse the minds of men. When the act of sin took place, death as they thought was to be physical at that very moment. Sin brought death to the human race, physically and spiritually, and the human race pays daily for the price for the sin of Adam. As we look around daily, we witness wars and rumors of wars, with great human death, hunger, murder of men, and of women and children. There is corruption on every level of government, because of the love of money, which is the root of all evil. For the unconverted as well as the converted these are some of the physical reaping because of sin. The spiritual aspect to the reaping of sin is the separation from God, which is more hurtful to the saved than physical death. The saved know, to be absent from the body, is to be present with the Lord. One sign of spiritual reaping is guilt, which will overtake a person's mind when he has sinned. We are aware, when we have done things not pleasing, in the eyesight of God; therefore, we try to hide our guilt with an outward appearance of our own righteousness. We also know sin is what causes us to be law-breakers, in the eyes of God. Let us reflect back to the statements, of those who will say 'I did not die, right then, when I did wrong'. The explanation for this statement is: Adam lived to be over nine hundred years old before physical death took him, but spiritual death the separation from God, happened the moment he disobeyed God.

Guilt, as mentioned before, plays an important role in man's relationship with God, because of sin. From the beginning to now, anyone who knows God, and has accepted Jesus as Lord and Savior, will enter into this area of guilt when he or she has sinned. The guilt surfaces, as one reads the Bible or hears the Word of God preached or taught. This illumination brings our spirit into closer contact with the Holy Spirit and conviction happens. Sinners know, in their hearts, when they have disobeyed God. The guilt of sin has allowed the devil to keep many in bondage and their relationship with God will move farther and farther away from God.

Those who are in this predicament will seek medical professionals for help and there will be some who will question their own sexuality. Those in this predicament will be led by the devil to form relationship with the same sex. This bondage of guilt will also lead some to take their own life. The answer to any predicament is to turn to God and trust Jesus to cleanse one from the sin of bondage. "If we confess our sins, He is faithful and just to forgive us our sins, and to cleanse us from all unrighteousness (I John1:9)."

Every person has failed to do what he ought to do, and it is only by the power of God one will be able to be removed from the bondage of guilt. We can sit around and continually blame everything on Adam as the usher in of sin into the human race, and rightly so, he has to take some blame. As Apostle Paul points out; shall we continue to sin that grace may abound? The man born in sin must take accountably for his own actions, just as Adam had to give account and make amends with God for his sin, so do we.

When one understands the gravity of sin he or she must confess their sins, so the devil will loose control, and the joy and happiness of serving God is restored. The person who suffers with guilt must understand he or she is not the only one who has had this feeling. The devil is working day and night to keep mankind in this type of thought process, which produces physical death and spiritual death.

Jonathan Edwards (1758) Christian doctrine of original sin points to the fact of universal reign of death because of sin. This is shown over and over with mankind for man was made to live a life of happiness. Death was not understood or known, at that time. The transgression of Adam, as all the writers give a viewpoint, and show that death is upon all sinful people and that we come into the world sinful. The sin of then and now has not changed over the years.

Jonathan Edwards makes a good argument with scriptural backing, in his beliefs of the Doctrine of Original Sin. His argument is that there is a universal sinfulness of mankind. Jonathan Edwards said, "All sin deserves and justly exposes to everlasting destruction, under the wrath and curse of God". To back up his belief he referred to (Gal.3:10) For as many as are of the works of the law are under the curse: for it is written. Cursed is ever one that continueth not in all things, which are written in the book of the law to do them. (Gal.3:22) But the scripture hath concluded all under sin, that the promise by faith of Jesus Christ might be given to them that believe. One can see, even those who tried to live by the Law and broke the law were sinners. Today, under grace one is a sinner. There is no escape from the sinful nature of men as long as the present nature of the First Adam is in us; therefore, it is by this one man sin entered into the human race.

Many will ask questions about the angels, and how they came into their sinful state, since God created them and they were made to serve God in Heaven? We can only surmise, they had a choice to obey and they chose to disobey just as man has done. Sin is a parasite and the meaning takes on different forms. The Millennium Online Digital Library shows the meaning of sin in Greek and Hebrew. If the word sin is typed into a search block, and all of the meanings come together, each definition of the word sin means to miss the mark the divine laws of God.

In this discussion of Sin Then and Now, man has fallen short and has tried for many years to reach back to God by his goodness, intellect, and money. The devil has easily deceived us and others around us! The hypocrisy of our thinking has prevented some from reaching to Jesus for restoration. The possessions of sin are so numerous, within mankind, even those who have great educations have failed to comprehend the severity and the results of it. God has demanded that sin has to be punished, yet he has provided restoration and fellowship for the sinner; whether, he is unconverted or converted. What the bullocks and turtle doves could not do to satisfy God, for the sins of old, the outward action of men today can not satisfy God either. The satisfaction, which God receives, is the whole atonement for sin. This had to be done, by His only Begotten Son Jesus Christ. "Jesus is the acceptable substitute for the sins of mankind", Lehman Strauss, Litt.D. F R. G .S, The Doctrine of Sin, (www.Bible. org).

There is a Hymn which says, what can wash away my sins, nothing but the blood of Jesus. To satisfy God, the blood of Jesus had to be shed. This pure blood is without any impurities "The sins of all of us were laid upon Christ". "The LORD hath laid on Him (Jesus Christ) the iniquity of us all" (Isa. 53:6). To those who believe we understand Christ's death satisfied the holiness of God. Christ came to earth not to be one to satisfy man's desire to be rich with material goods this is not to say he will not bless us to have wealth but his advent to earth was to give mankind wealth in salvation and this is by dying for the sins of man.

God could not forgive sin because of man's goodness, for there is not one who could put a claim on perfection and there is not one who could put a claim on goodness, to do this would be contrary to His Word.

Human sin has to be punished by God, because of who God is. God does not want any to perish, for his love for mankind will never cease; however, God's divine perfection prevents him from having a close relationship with moral evil. Let none think he or she can do what they want and still have a relationship with God. The greatest example of separation, because of sin, is Christ upon the cross who is perfect. God, for a split moment, withdrew himself from his Son as He saw the sin of mankind upon him. Shouldn't men cry the cry of Jesus, 'My God, My God why hast thou forsaken me?', when we do not feel the presence of God in our lives when we have sinned against God. It is upon all men, regardless of race, creed or color, to cry 'My God, My God.

One can surmise, sin has trapped men and has shut their mouths from crying My God, has sin hindered their speech, has sin removed this cry from their language? To some we must say yes, this darkness of sin, which many live in is blinding them from seeing the light Jesus has provided by his death for our sins. Many have also turned deaf ears to the Gospel and its connotation to the human race. Many have looked upon this Savior as just another person who came to start trouble. I must agree to a certain extent. He came to trouble the soul of men with the Truth, to trouble the spirit of men in regard to their sinfulness, and to trouble men's deprived hearts.

Sin Then and Now will always be troubled, by Jesus and his atonement. Let us who are faithful never forget to remind those who are faced with total separation from God to seek the Salvation He brings. Let us who are saved, by no means, forget how we once were lost, but now we are found. Those who stay in their sinful state will have no peace and no calmness of the soul, until there is a turn around to the goodness of God and repent of their sins. To do this God will take their sins and cast them into the sea of forgetfulness never to be brought up again.

We must explain to the carnal Christian and to the unsaved, there is protection from the wrath of God when it comes to sinful acts, even nations who think their generosity to others prevents them for facing the wrath of God. People must look within themselves and their sinful state, for they also will reap the fruit of their labor, which will lead to total separation into the lake of fire. Today's man will still try to cover up his sinful act by trying to put his sins into segment. Many will say to themselves, little sin, big sin, white lie and etc. yet their understanding about the consequence of their sin has escaped their thought process and these little sin-doers, as well as the big sin-doers will have to reap what they sow. The bible teaches sin is sin and there is no such thing as a person escaping the penalty of sin whether it's big or little. Sin has caused some to think they are pros at doing evil, going against a Holy God. Many have developed the attitude they want get caught for their actions, but they have failed to understand God knows all sees all.

If Adams could speak, he would say to them, 'I thought I could hide from a Holy God, but I failed to realize, He made me and it was His garden I was trying to hide in, it was his leaves I tried to cover myself with, so how could I get away with something from one who is all knowing?'. Let none be mistaken, God is still in charge, and not us. For man to witness the glory of God in his dwelling place called Heaven he first must come to grip within himself the sinful nature he carries can be overcome, he must relinquish himself to the power of God and his plan for mankind.

Conclusion: Look into the Bible sinful man, and believe the Word of God. We must observe and see the downward spiral of God's chosen people and observe how He was always warning them of the consequences of sinful acts and showing them the results of sin in their lives. Observe, if you will, the progression of sin as they reject the goodness of God and failed to observe and obey His divine laws. Look sinful man and read, in the Holy writing of God His plan to save man from His wrath. I must say, if there is no confession of sin, if there is no repentance of sin, if there is no faith in the birth, death and resurrection of His son Jesus Christ, God has one choice, which is to totally separate himself from the unbeliever.

Let the sinner beware, sin is the destroying factor to anything, which ails man. Sin is the reason God has pronounced judgment upon the human race and sin is the reason God sent His Son to bridge the gap between Him and mankind. To those who accept Jesus Christ as Lord and Savior, the gap has been closed and the way to God has been opened. The way to heaven, which will be our future home, has already been prepared by Jesus. All of our sins have been forgiven, through the atonement by Jesus Christ. We must not forget sin still lurks in the darkness to engulf us; as long as this nature of the first Adam is still present, sin will be present. But thanks be to God for the Second Adam who spoke 'Behold, I make all things new (Rev.21:5).' What a blessing it will be, for the Sin of Then and the Sins of Now, they will be no more. The Sins of Then and Now will be cast into the Lake of Fire with those who enjoyed the desires of them. The Sins of Then and Now will not trouble man anymore. The conditions, which God began in the beginning of time, will be restored back to its former state. This blessing, which all believers will receive, will never be tainted by sin and the viewpoints of the devil. So let those who have been saved from the penalty of sin, which is death, sing a song of rejoicing 'Come now Lord Jesus Come Now'. Amen.

References

1. Chapter 17-Doctrine of Sin: Sin from a Biblical Perspective. Retrieved April 17,2006 from www. pbministries.org/Theology/simmons/chapter17. htm

2. Edwards, J. Christian Doctrine of Original Sin. (1758). Retrieved April15, 2006 from http://www. jonathanedwards.com/text/osin/osin.htm

3. Millennium Online Digital Library. http://odl. mdivs.edu/login.cgi?requestedURL=/

4. Scofield,C. (1980).26 Great Words:Scofield Bible Correspondence Course/Moody.

5. Strauss, L. The Doctrine of Sin. Retrieved April 18, 2006 from http://bible.org/page. asp?page_id=399

6. The Doctrine of Sin-its need in the Church by Dr. Ken Matto. Retrieved April 12, 2006 from http://www,scionofzion.com/sin.htm